I0843357

SILLY ALIEN MONSTERS

COLORING BOOK

BY
HILLROCKS COLORING BOOK

How To Use This Book:

1. Just color the way you feel like

2. Have fun

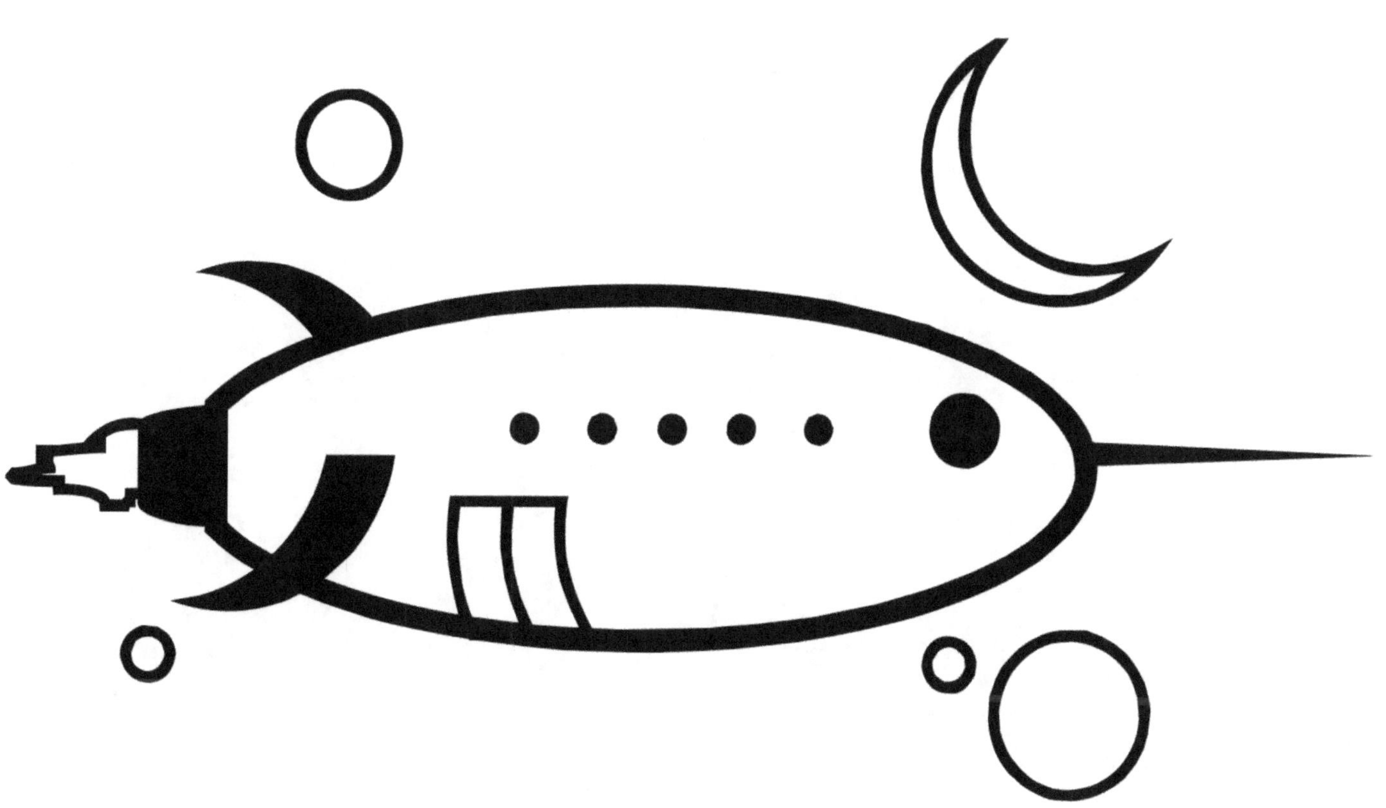

The end of the book

Stay Creative!

www.ingramcontent.com/pod-product-compliance
Lightning Source LLC
Chambersburg PA
CBHW081630250726
48657CB00009B/2814